Free Verse Editions

Edited by Jon Thompson

BLADE WORK

Lily Brown

Winner of the New Measure Poetry Prize

Parlor Press
Anderson, South Carolina
www.parlorpress.com

Parlor Press LLC, Anderson, South Carolina, 29621

Library of Congress Cataloging-in-Publication Data on File

978-1-64317-498-3 (paperback)
978-1-64317-499-0 (pdf)
978-1-64317-500-3 (ePub)

1 2 3 4 5

Cover image: "Bird Cloud" by Lyonel Feininger. Harvard Art Museums.
© 2024 Artists Rights Society (ARS), New York / VG Bild-Kunst, Bonn.
Used by permission.

Book design by David Blakesley.

Parlor Press, LLC is an independent publisher of scholarly and trade titles in
print and multimedia formats. This book is available in paperback and ebook
formats from Parlor Press on the World Wide Web at https://www.parlorpress.
com or through online and brick-and-mortar bookstores. For submission
information or to find out about Parlor Press publications, write to Parlor
Press, 3015 Brackenberry Drive, Anderson, South Carolina, 29621, or email
editor@parlorpress.com.

Contents

Contents

For Charlie and Cora

Blade Work

Also, Who laid the Rainbow's piers,
Also, Who leads the docile spheres
By withes of supple blue?

—Emily Dickinson

Venus Transit

I heard the voice of reason
swerve boneward as it mouthed
the high hills of Art.
I know both sides:
the violence of artifact
and the living tree,
airy branches full of weeds.
Once a sitting thing in a thing
that stuck me back, I walk
straight out in heavy rain,
trying not to aim,
his lungs gum-thick,
each word towed out with a chain
pulled simultaneously back.
I make another motion,
send a jagged gift.

Days are dams.
Each week posts
a sign above the water.
This week: Goodbye.
Last week: The Possible.
I close the dam of The Possible,
open the dam of Goodbye.
Its aperture is a mouth
pasted mostly shut.
Through welding glass,
see astral green.
I look for freckle Venus.
It's gone, or on the blurred brink of sun.

These days, dream is a terror
unromantic to disclose.
Take up its visions like fruit in arms.
Forget them in the cold barrel of the sun.

The Simple Hill

Black path, skinny statues. Each step up,
you throw a rock out with your voice,
a pebble, a jagged fragment of slate.

With each, you use your body
to admit what's wrong.
You describe the problem
as milestones, and your

milestones breathe. So you go north.
You make your air different.
And in that split you glimpse
the simple hill, its retinal gleam.

You think to bounce your voice
off the simple hill to see if it's
a mirror or a box of breath.

I Tie Down My Fill, Close the Sky

When I went outside and spoke, metal
was coming out of my skin.
I spoke backwards and others
rotated the phrases back for me.
I called for comfort, asking
for something pliable and holy.
I'd sleep here in your crescent
eye, the laughter phasing from your face.
However strange we need to be to get there.
The skin's scales speak of failure.
Easy to fail all day. I'm only
drawing a shape, the way
the dandelion seeds get blown up
or out, crushed down but still taprooted,
a center, an estimation of the present,
what's swelling in the body this fine
hot day, irises blooming, dogs cruising
planets as they mash their bodies
against each other, chin-quaking
out of the understory. What's trying?
Trying's what we cut through, the dogs
horsing in the bush, the duck's sudden clang,
or even thick leaves leaning up.
I kneel like some other birth outside
buildings. Purpose falls, too, via gravity's tool.
I push wood from wood, study the spider
davening in its casual sleep,
its body a light switch turning off off off.

Blue Machine

Shelves of cloud stacked down.
Then the brighter break.
The mountain's dirty load.

The building's touch gives
the wind its pitch.

And experience?
The critic sharp upon abstraction?
Anything's that.

How *C* bends the hand or hisses out
from teeth and tongue.
The soft craft of these heavy clouds
is wet in the fist.

And the boat I'm watching rock across
the range—a blue machine that breaks
and opens, breaks and opens

The Difference We Make in What We See

1

So begins the night, combed back
into the body, then braided over
the body, it seals the drumbeats in.

2

I unfold fingers, bend knee, turn hip away from tree.
Outside, dark bodies join their voices.
We throb to be relieved.

3

A woman asks me, *is* _____ *a real word?*
It is, but if the mind doesn't discern it, no
need to believe.

4

Figures remembered at the table:
one glazed eye, one neck tipped down,
one tugging at salad with a tuning fork.

5

In this version of time, I hold a horsehair
bow, feel it hard with my hands.
I would dream up the *where* but it's gone,
only crusted time felt with the body just now.

6

We enter the museum of masks.
The front advances, crossing plank.
Our photos: gates we open backwards
to draw the way the mind erases.

7

Do we have to go into the pantry face-first,
traced with choc-thick milk, all night long
in the house limned with click song?

8

Sometimes, August, we'd lie in the one
air-conditioned room, stretched flat,
the dead dropping heat.

Space-time parceled out, flower by gloved
hand, house by sea.

9

Even the car's curve through corridor of pine.
Even heedless hum can't break green brawn.

10

A pasture's deep color proves immune to point of view.

The Natural World

He drew dirty
flowers, then clayey
flowers. Then mint

against gray. Trees
look like legs
beneath low clouds.

Blooms implode
up close, mucked
with color.

Handles for the landscape:
sea scraped
of water, sketch with

hidden humans.
All skeletons
look alike—their walking

stick bones, their
achromatized
privacy.

Thirty-Five

There are so many ways
to be told who one is and

so few ways to be real.
My friend coolly breaks

the rules of poetry.
The sky closes.

I take off my rainy sneakers
so the sun can burn

my back through the window,
so I can lie

on the brown couch
imagining revenge.

Why bother
with letters that birthed

that old foe hope?

Against all word to the contrary,
we are permanently children.

The sky with its vast clouds
is more beautiful than shutting

up the glow,
than drawing a thin lattice

about your life.

Field Figure

Her body twists at the waist
still comfortably intact.
Any world reverses. Earth on sky,
black on grey, urchins
in flowers, i.e. the field
is the sea, an iris
sun redone.

The moon's not cratered but seeded.

Body parts obscured by feather.
Body parts made circle by snakes.
Feather, flower, feather, flush.
Sky all lisping stars.
Lux is a measure of luminous flux.

Eyes, half shut, dim studs.

I make a bed—white covers white covers
checkered dog,
green book half gone.
At mind's light
the ceiling's a sea heaving.

Aquatic on hind legs
the sea watches,
the striped prairie, hung with hearts, eyes.

I watch sight regular
in the garden,
in the garden
watch it move
so many seeds from the iris sun.

                    after Cristina Toro's *The Invisible Life of Small Things*

From a Downeast Porch

Dog body dropped into place
in sun, in shade, by the rocking
chair's blade.

Dog body, six slats wide.
White birds round a boat
like a chime

mirror the fisher who
mirrors white birds.

Once, I saw an osprey
sputter cross-sky,
too-heavy fish in its claws.

Rocking to nursery
lines, cormorant wing
blades beat

their blue runway.

Sugar Pine

There's a sugar pine on a hill
in Ogunquit, an interloper
among leafless thickets

spilling birdsong
down tricked rocks.
The sugar pine leans

nearly onto the house
whose view it obstructs,
precarious and ragged

under the clouds'
dusky lid. Despite
its proximity

to me, the house, the sky
and all, the sugar pine's
alone, astonishingly so.

Socket

Out of a ripped situation, we learned
to boat. Tacked once the harbor
in a wood-ribbed float
then curved to port.

I remember twirling through air,
a baton in pain, then an arm
backed into its socket
by a doctor.

Knocked into structure,
I open my bones. I could
go about it
differently, but what good

is rattling in a basket?
And is it waiting
if you don't know
after is what you'd want?

Salton Sea

Seagrass spears dim wind, green
velocity's serrated fin.

About the sated sea.
About the bone-glass beach.
We want a fish's soft
bones of belief,

bright white smells
I open eyes wide to believe
anything is glass—white striped black,
the chemical breeze.

Here's a phantasm in tropic paint:
an egret wheeling
into god's metal wing.

At the Hospital

no knives, no
mirrors. Prominent

men framing
windows

aren't aluminum,
are made of glass.

Inside prism windows,
trees point

up, their roots
sized to cut glass.

We Dug Diamonds

in the dirt behind the house.
The myth was a map

a pedestrian walked.
We glued her voice

to our legs, took the dirt in.
The everyday is the bottom

of my shoes, what I screw
to the floorboards.

It's our bodies doing
time for time

we couldn't become.

Might Be Round but Appears Smooth

We have new neighbors. Bikes tilt under
lean-to of darkness. Sounds
bump out. I copy someone's
disjointed beat.

I think he took his notes, scrambled them
on the mud-footed field,
and one hook-shaped leaf after leaf,
turning, failed to fix an other.

This is my dream of falling through black,
the train now baying its entrance.
This is what I mean. I mean what I mean.
For she who takes up likeness

and throws it down, the screen whines
open like a dog.

Somnambulent Crescendo

A crow's publicity reinstates the real.

I believe it, but where's electricity's

fizz? Is it, the world?

Your markings compose a cape,

divide your back;

into its hallway I move.

This painting goes all the way back.

Natural Bridge

Dark boats the cove.

I away to it, eyes where we are.
Trees aren't one, they depend.

We're the map's
lines when we lack technologic.

*

Then a tree flaps,
a tree haloes the moon,

the moon blinks off.

Around here

there's the present,

and then
there's anything else.

Out Here

We drive in one thin silver take
through blue heat
in a squat silver tank.
I don't know what
casts shadows,
the lumps of the range
too far ahead,
a cloud's torn edge.
When I paint the mountains
dark or clear blue, it looks deliberate,
like I meant to drape light more or less
heavily over the high terrain.
Like I'm managing
a small ocean, I think
while filling the ice-cube tray,
or with my head in your armpit,
during dinner clean up,
or when I'm alone but can smell you.

This morning I wake, sit
on the deck, close my eyes.
Wild turkeys are claps of thunder
over a nearby tree thick
with bird sound. When I open
my eyes, a family unfurls,
five or six necks bud
out of high grass and run,
each with one eye on me, away.
Then I walk in the heat and wind,
squat to listen to my sister's hard day,
turn left up the hill.
Layers of sagebrush front the hills,
gathering far blue
mountains and the loops
of my shoelaces around them.

There's one telephone pole
out here, attached to nothing.
I send a letter, a postcard, plant them
in the mailbox, turn the red flag up.
Every night, my dreams are
nightmares or reveries,
losses or gifts.
Riding a turquoise cruiser,
I hear a thump and make out
two forearms and half a face
against a narrow window.
As I pass, a sandhill crane expels
a chain from its throat,
sounds the metallic
insult of my presence. I look up
'presence' in the thesaurus and
read *The presence of the train was
indicated electrically.*

It may as well say, *There was*
obvious chemistry between
the train and the track or
The bicycle ran under blood power.
I push past a small snake,
dead or so deeply lost
in sun it looks gone.
Outside the window,
a trees' branches form
a circle, a line of smaller
trees below, birds raining
through the aperture.
A truck heaves by, its engine
ringing like a beaten bell.
I wake with my left thumb
in my left ear and a bright sore
spot where memory should be.

No matter. Day is a dream I
read through the flat
streets of the page
outside your house,
and you keep moving
through the novel's rooms.
At dinner, I hear a man
tell a woman the presidential
frontrunner is a megalomaniac
because *How many times does
her husband have to cheat on her?*
You asked if people pair
with opposites because it works.
All I know is that you open
places others shut.
Pushed up against
the tunicate-encrusted dock,
I watch you swim
two ropes from a knot.

Academia

Driving the round road, I instruct myself.

We are fingers, we are bridged by bodies.

The buildings here are red and clap
all over the horizon.

Transparency

Branches press flat on glass.
Down the street, semaphores.

Heavy jugs of light
judder at crossroads

close to elegant until a picture
points them out.

All day I splinter leaves
with my feet, conduct them

in, singed flags.
I think I see you in the back window,

waving there, your show moving
west then east.

Torso turns to see

how great a distance
I earned to make.

Taxonomic

I saw the bird throat
like a toad
billow out; thought

to take a picture
and send it.
I swallowed the door-

jamb's shine. The threshold
breaks off as I use it.
The water has a breeze

says the dog-eared lady
who owns both.
The ripples

sit down flat on the pond.

House Home

If something outside the mind
makes the mind—

I'd rather a ceiling wet with river,
the elemental basement,
cement's slick grit.

Up on the gusty terrace,
experimental glass takes yellow

light down into
its purple middle and
fits it in cellar grey.

At the bottom stair,
I play the alchemical fan

and its pedals
wing the composite up.

Form

The wrinkling in my peripheral
vision repeats. What's moving?

Not the building, its bodies.
The river beside.

So close we're
almost in it?

That'd be another state,
limbs in liquid, rock-dented.

Crushed a dead moth with my sleeve.
Anywhere I lean, wing.

Figurative Love

The tent's a sheet with a man under it.
An open-faced lover, vision's trick.
The haptic cold.
Go sick into it.
What's the story?
Solids pushing me hard,
or my imagined hands
pushing hard on solids?

Whichever sea we can set,
an iced-up crate of spray
saved for later, skins
shading away.
I run these thoughts down
like a list each night.
In the morning, they're still here.

Certain Allied Experiments

To be very young and beached on a couch.
Describe this feeling as rubber,
warm to the touch,
lodged in the chest.
In a cabin in the mountains, see bluish fog
or the rogue sky coming
through cloud
to dislodge stone habit. *To stand by*
stood up against *surprise*—
a valve that lets another consciousness arrive.
For a figurine slung from the ceiling
see a fat-bellied hen, see a flat fish,
a glassed leaf, a blinking desert built,
like tonight, out of lightning.
I'm on a mountain, rocking in its side.

Documentarian

A storm rolls color around
the mountaintop, sky given over
to the deeply hued.
The river, stirred to sultry,
carves the village up.

Night figures a doorjamb's red
square. Light above cuts
its stage into a scene.

So what?

I know looking and not
pinning the view.

I've been hum-stuck, parallel
to the woodwork,
saying *um*.

How close to the body
should you hold your hands
when the view pulses, when with each
beat you change
what's in or in front of you?

Trashed or Tied

Six white windows slit night
open to its emptiness.

What do you read on its canvas?

What pulled you here
(burnt air) cools itself
in the river's basin,
smudges sunup.

Someone's finger says
of the local skyline
smoke there.

Then fog dispenses with street.

Which would you prefer,
the manhandled garden
or the monstrous
dandelion out of its head?

The Complete Poems

Give some back to the mapland.
Material qualities, stammering
repetition. More interested
in atmosphere, leaf and cloud,
than clock-like architecture's alarms.
The speaking weed points to her heart splitting.
Sure of himself, he's a stand of columns.
Elements make them age.
Attention may transform
time = days = circles.
The objects are lively, contrived—
Stevens' bucks, Moore's catalogues.
Pretty clattering of birds and wives.
Fish finally uncompared to flowers,
the book's gold fertilizes corpses.
By exporting the personal "we,"
the moon could be removed.
Why try seeing sun "the other way around"?
Thunder is a child,
the fence is thinking.
The bird is a bird
made by a human all the same.

after Elizabeth Bishop

The Difficult Rightness

Out of riverbank, a blue pipe grows
long, glares white, an artificial song.
The wind runs by, taken up by river water light.

Like glue in air it glows.
Branches stretch over soil-strapped
stems, their bright dials spun up.

Before we stop, long thorax clapped to
metal mesh, a painter's tight triangles
diffuse under mask of blue.

One pulls the other. Cloudy color tugs
and covers. So the ferns, bowed bridges,
tip down to flesh our fossil necks.

Commute

Pass through bombed-out
shrubs, feathered extrusions,
greenish metal cut to square
and sky.

Is this the jungle?
A rain-wide paddock
gathers water,

the word *Up*'s thumbed
onto a pilement
beside a grove
of eucalyptus graves.

The hand, the arm,
the shoulder—stumps
or system?

Wind Wake

The blinds don't move
when wind's an iris rising.

*

Caught in a current,
the last raisin leaves
are put down for winter.

*

I look at a photo
of dense clover—
it doesn't move.

*

Not even the chalky back
of an eyelid twitching
moves me.

*

The blind's shadow
like an itch across the wall bends
around a corner. Into the open eye
its light comes
and I take it.

All Week Light

howls through the hill.
Beneath it, clarity slips

this shelter—
foggy, lucent—
glass bent in a storm

of sun. I'm not finished
but for this wall of world
waiting to yield. It's hard

letting sand
into the body. I can't

shake honey
out of my veins.

After Susan Rothenberg's *Untitled Drawing, No. 41, 1977*

The horse gallops
fog under its chin,
behind a hind leg,
haze in parts erased.
The smudge in the body's
portioned air. Darwin
threw lizards
by the tail
into the ocean
to find out if they swim.
The unlitigious sea
iguana shrinks
its skeleton when
algae's scarce and man's
finger bones revolve
in briny light. I was thinking
we'll have no other year
to traipse through
apple glut in the orchard,
in whose corridors
we ran through vegetal
waste, that rot that washed
my life of fog.

Sky Behind

Train-culled white
aluminum, lengths

of palm tree, haze-
wrapped hill

en route to sky behind.

Or inside, looking at a bumper
sticker: *Warning:*

Driver may be jerking off.
Now a tangent

rolling down an off-ramp
crosses into motion.

Moon When the Cherries Turn Black

Overheard musing on the street
about the taxidermied dead,
I'm told *It's a cow moose*
before he asks permission

to humiliate me later. Later,
Did you see the red burning orb? I did,
and then collected with a camera
a pin's head for power.

A woman practices lassoing
before a door I need to enter.
Beyond her, rows of saddles
mellow in the glare.

As I falter there, another says
It's safe to go now,
while the first turns away
her folded face.

Water's Wild Nest

In a dream I escape through foliage,
and down a trail my father made,

with my mother and my father.

But for the obvious fact
of our being pursued,
I'm awed, wadding air

up in my fists to stuff
the cut where shards

don't know themselves
as anything but shattered.

What Are Maps

Thunder thuds out of
plum clouds. The gate
to the highest point
I climb locks with a chain
and two slots. One catches
two loops in its claw.
The other's a single blunt dent.
I can open it if I concentrate.
(A cow can't and that's
the point.) I once absorbed
a person so completely
recollection dimmed to grades
of light, mouths like cagey
gates. General and particular
rhymed to dream's interior.
This morning a wasp climbed
sticky onto a paintbrush
and reached one leg through
the air like a test. I didn't know
if it was faded or frozen
and nudged it to a navy book
then out the open door,
from which it went.
Hard work has an end
where it's not met. I will not,
for example, trail the leery fawn
who admits her face to query,
looks long, then runs.

The Hem of the Starry Curtain

The atmosphere looked split when low
clouds leaked sunlight, coming

from the west as if hauled
from a too-deep pool, a vein of sunset

twined through a bite of sky.
On the lawn, a rabbit stalled,

not twitching, a statue in ink
before a government hall.

Cloud drama's tacked
to you, also not twitching,

your palm filled with a future
named *not now*.

You hate p.m.'s lack of song,
how birdcall gets cuffed to

a scene so steady
it's nearly empty

but for that crane's ribcage
lifting from a vase of plain.

In Idaho

a deer squatted in the river.
We drove through ungreen
mountains, a tree glowing
black by the highway,
flames carved up by rivers
filled with brown trout
and sucker fish, their mouths
reliving riverbed. We
nudged them with trinkets
they ignored, swooning
through fireless water,
American firelight
a kind of twilight, a sack
of flammable stars.
Aerial photos flush pink,
as if a chemical sunset
stuffed in a cloud
burned through it.

Genetic

Delicate, genetic, the flowers
arrayed in fabrics sloping
from center, a series of tongues
but another movement, swaying
like hair unattached on the underside,
ends held at the axis.

Speaking of mothers, there are
paragraphs emerging, rectangular,
the ladder down to a green
dream underground—
I held a rung with one hand,
the other stuck between my knees.
Panicked, I thought I'd fall from
that form, in grief untwisted.

Trustchange.edu

What kind of silence is this?
One where I've invented
a telephone, a conversation
and a pause within it
that I'm smiling into before asking,
what kind of silence is this?

Trying to attach,
I loft iron from dirt
the day a man yelled
at a luffing sail and, unimpressed,
I had an instinct to yell back.
Or when I was blocked, hours
before nightfall, by several closed doors
and the babysitter and the howling heat that followed.

Where am I going?
The answer, it turns out, is an abyss.
Not so black as the one in that old dream
through which I fell
but one that has its formlessness.
So I scratch a path in snow
and through that un-lidded
pasture, summer.

Maybe we're mounted
in a rural museum, rippling
lawns of grasshopper busts,
icy marble floors.
This would be in Tulsa—I've been—
and in that future,
a freezing past.

One poet writes, *Trust's not trust until
its test.* The radio chirps, *Change your life—
santaclarauniversity.edu/change.*
Change not change
until its trust.

Rural museum, half crafted,
half arranged in memory's chain.
I've arrived, then, at the page of recollections,
picked from a small book in the pastoral night,

in the latter hem of darkness nearing morning
when I needed voice, the physical fact
against memory's airy commerce—
a hand that is a garden put to bed.

Past Noon in the Municipal Library

I sketch a bird
that turns squirrel,
its bones too broad
for avian form.

Hint of a nose,
scratch for a leg,
its chin points
at obvious wind.

Gone Sonnets

When I arrive, the library's spilling
a park from its lip.

Each birch root's stuffed
with three trunks. A ukulele,

two girls, and two young women
float notes over a white tent

filled with tense white chairs.
The amphitheater's levels

would seem to leverage sound
and space, if not for their tonal

waste. Next morning,
my neighbors sit to text

while discussing the relative
number of talkers

on the library's top
and bottom floors.

(I entered the upper field,
hollowed from the middle out,

a gong-less bell.) Meanwhile,
people crowd the cellar,

below the upper tower,
gossiped into an era.

Hedgehogs of Instagram

The caption advises
reading up on hedgehogs
before adopting "this shy
eleven-month-old."
In the photo, the hedgehog's
nose is pale pink,
its back curved
against opening.
The feeling of being lost
alongside the thought
that one must supply
a literal equivalent to feeling.
These are dark works
stemming in the skull,
jamming the pen against
the whiteness of mind.

Essential Vagary

Woke to the intention of quiet
there are wheezing birds, relentless
water from the lion-mouthed spigot.

My dream: I ran a marathon
with high school classmates,
men who fought about their wives

while dodging trucks. A vast lawn
of runners lay down
at a street crossing, waiting

for traffic to break. Politicians
jogged by in monk's robes.
Grades would never matter again.

While my peers ran on I
ate rice crispy treats and drank
nectarine-infused water.

Soft fruit floated to the top
and I drank it, rapt at
the crossing, sweet in my mouth.

Reading *Paterson*

Of the doctor's vernacular
I have no doubt
he was schooled
in his words, but
in anatomical silhouette
his women seem faulted
for every salacious
scene into which
he deposits a man
through a slot.
The rooster's comb,
the water's comb,
both appear to me plaited
over the ocean's plain,
hardly objects, yet I've
found a glossary online
that collects Atlantic
bric-a-brac "by reason
of an act of man."
Doesn't the author
know the sea upon
some gimbaled struts
is not what I want?

As in Repeating Autumnal Dreams

The mold man suits up.
Wet air blown into
the overspace meets
its galactic end.

Today I am paint cans, land-
scaping, processing a melon.
The last of the hurricane
blows its rainy
eruptions through.

Like a warm room
where stuff slowly
lifts unto the air,
I feel sometimes spacious.

I can blow the floating
world into the forest
to hover above
the sandy stream still
moving, like a magnet,

west. Darkness, its attendant
wallowing, its legs
flattening slowly
to October ground.

I saw a pink spider
admire the billow
of its legs in summer glory,
the corners of my house

all waving glossy
webs at me as I open
every window, then shut
their crackly joints.

Mourning through Sunlight

Here at the stonewilled farmhouse,
hewed to each stranger's
rules, with several flies
I hover the rooms humming,
wings whirring, motor-
organ's buzzing broken finally
into an oval cry as the baying
hounds start up
(*Fragile*, the sign says,
Do not touch),
and I'm bonded to the woods
not to hunt, but to be,
having counted from one hundred
to one, asleep. So my dream
of illegal sound, produced
by us in love and trust,
flayed open by a detective's
pointy talk. And the woman
who picks peaches reached
their tree from a tightrope
in the lone blue
silence that turns,
late afternoon,
as the weather staggers on.

Blade Work

I went many years without
reading the listings. I wanted
to be liked by the poet
in the dank restaurant
who fastened his face
to its shadows. There was an aura
of mock wood, pebbles
I aligned to stay true to
some cracked intuition.
Somewhere in the cyber
ether, an alarum.
The dirtiest place in your home
has been revealed—the blare
above a kitchen sink
while I clean my teeth.
Lear uses the royal *we*
while addressing his daughters,
who press their breasts
to the floor, whose collarbones

nick stone. While I was out
with the dog, a raccoon
bent its head around
the corner store's bright
wall and stared. Last week
I burst a green balloon
with the Outback's black
back wheel. Still earlier,
I stood in a field of old
harvest shards. Birds rose
then fell through their
own shattered feathers
for the sleek dog to retrieve.
Clippets of summer lawns,
I misread in Doug's book,
proceeding to dream
of chlorophyll debutantes
shucked from the earth's
round edge, cut
mercifully away from
the semi-automatic sun.

Acknowledgments

Thank you to the editors of the following publications in which these poems, sometimes in slightly different forms, first appeared: *6X6, Aesthetix, Apartment Poetry, A Bad Penny Review, A Public Space, Boston Review, Cannibal, Catch Up Literary Journal, Dusie/Tuesday Poem, Green Humanities, Jubilat, Lana Turner, Marco Polo Quarterly, Maiden Magazine, Mississippi Review, MUSE/A Journal, Oversound, Sink Review, The Offending Adam, Tuba, WASHTKS*, and *Whiskey Island*.

"Socket" won the Poetry Society of America's 2012 Cecil Hemley Memorial Award.

Several of these poems first appeared in the chapbook *The Haptic Cold* (Ugly Duckling Presse, 2013). Thank you to everyone at Ugly Duckling, particularly Katherine Bogden Bayard.

Thank you to Arte Studio Ginestrelle, the Ucross Foundation, and the Vermont Studio Center for residencies during which many of these poems were written.

Notes

The title "Moon When the Cherries Turn Black" is borrowed from the book *Black Elk Speaks: The Complete Edition*, by John G. Neihardt.

"Trustchange.edu" borrows the language "trust's not trust until / its test" from the poem "Siren Test" by Robyn Schiff.

"Reading *Paterson*" borrows the phrase "by reason of an act of man" from "A Glossary of Coastal Engineering Terms," published by the U.S. Government Printing Office.

"Blade Work" includes a misreading of the line "clippings of a summer lawn" from D.A. Powell's poem "[simple endings overlap: grief is interference]."

Thank you to friends, fellow writers, and teachers who either read and commented on earlier versions of these poems, sometimes many years ago, or who offered encouragement and camaraderie: Charlie Black, Joanna Penn Cooper, Graham Foust, Brenda Hillman, Angela Hume, Joseph Massey, Sara Mumolo, Jennifer Nelson, Ed Pavlić, D.A. Powell, Susan Rosenbaum, Dan Rosenberg, Catherine Theis, Emma Winsor Wood, and Andrew Zawacki. Thank you to my classmates at the University of Georgia and to the Saint Mary's College MFA Program's community of writers. And finally, thanks to the friends who make a writing life feel possible: Allie Foster, Allen Frost, and Adam Morris.

About the Author

Lily Brown is the author of *Rust or Go Missing* (Cleveland State University Poetry Center) and several chapbooks, including *The Haptic Cold* (Ugly Duckling Presse). Her poems have appeared in *American Letters and Commentary, A Public Space, Boston Review, Colorado Review, Denver Quarterly, Gulf Coast, Lana Turner, Mississippi Review*, and *Oversound*, among others. She has won the Poetry Society of America's Cecil Hemley Memorial Award and has been awarded residencies at Arte Studio Ginistrelle, the Vermont Studio Center, and the UCross Foundation. She lives in Maine with her family and works as a writing teacher.

Photograph of the author by
Charlie Black. Used by permission.

Free Verse Editions

Edited by Jon Thompson

13 ways of happily by Emily Carr
& in Open, Marvel by Felicia Zamora
& there's you still thrill hour of the world to love by Aby Kaupang
Alias by Eric Pankey
the atmosphere is not a perfume it is odorless by Matthew Cooperman
At Your Feet (A Teus Pés) by Ana Cristina César, edited by
    Katrina Dodson, trans. by Brenda Hillman and Helen Hillman
Bari's Love Song by Kang Eun-Gyo, translated by Chung Eun-Gwi
Between the Twilight and the Sky by Jennie Neighbors
Blade Work by Lily Brown
Blood Orbits by Ger Killeen
The Bodies by Christopher Sindt
The Book of Isaac by Aidan Semmens
The Calling by Bruce Bond
Canticle of the Night Path by Jennifer Atkinson
Child in the Road by Cindy Savett
Civil Twilight by Giles Goodland
Condominium of the Flesh by Valerio Magrelli, trans. by Clarissa Botsford
Contrapuntal by Christopher Kondrich
Country Album by James Capozzi
Cry Baby Mystic by Daniel Tiffany
The Curiosities by Brittany Perham
Current by Lisa Fishman
Day In, Day Out by Simon Smith
Dear Reader by Bruce Bond
Dismantling the Angel by Eric Pankey
Divination Machine by F. Daniel Rzicznek
Elsewhere, That Small by Monica Berlin
Empire by Tracy Zeman
Erros by Morgan Lucas Schuldt
Extinction of the Holy City by Bronisław Maj, trans. by Daniel Bourne
Fifteen Seconds without Sorrow by Shim Bo-Seon, trans. by
    Chung Eun-Gwi and Brother Anthony of Taizé
The Forever Notes by Ethel Rackin
The Flying House by Dawn-Michelle Baude
General Release from the Beginning of the World by Donna Spruijt-Metz
Ghost Letters by Baba Badji

Go On by Ethel Rackin
Here City by Rick Snyder
I Am Not Korean by Song Kyeong-dong
An Image Not a Book by Kylan Rice
Instances: Selected Poems by Jeongrye Choi, trans. by Brenda Hillman,
  Wayne de Fremery, & Jeongrye Choi
Invitatory by Molly Spencer
Last Morning by Simon Smith
The Magnetic Brackets by Jesús Losada, trans. by M. Smith & L. Ingelmo
Man Praying by Donald Platt
A Map of Faring by Peter Riley
The Miraculous Courageous by Josh Booton
Mirrorforms by Peter Kline
M O 月 N by Chengru He
A Myth of Ariadne by Martha Ronk
No Shape Bends the River So Long by Monica Berlin & Beth Marzoni
North | Rock | Edge by Susan Tichy
Not into the Blossoms and Not into the Air by Elizabeth Jacobson
Overyellow, by Nicolas Pesquès, translated by Cole Swensen
Parallel Resting Places by Laura Wetherington
pH of Au by Vanessa Couto Johnson
Physis by Nicolas Pesquès, translated by Cole Swensen
Pilgrimage Suites by Derek Gromadzki
Pilgrimly by Siobhán Scarry
Poems from above the Hill & Selected Work by Ashur Etwebi, trans. by
  Brenda Hillman & Diallah Haidar
The Prison Poems by Miguel Hernández, trans. by Michael Smith
Puppet Wardrobe by Daniel Tiffany
Quarry by Carolyn Guinzio
remanence by Boyer Rickel
Republic of Song by Kelvin Corcoran
Rumor by Elizabeth Robinson
Saint with a Peacock Voice by L. S. Klatt
Settlers by F. Daniel Rzicznek
A Short History of Anger by Joy Manesiotis
Signs Following by Ger Killeen
Small Sillion by Joshua McKinney
Split the Crow by Sarah Sousa
Spine by Carolyn Guinzio
Spool by Matthew Cooperman
Strange Antlers by Richard Jarrette

A Suit of Paper Feathers by Nate Duke
Summoned by Guillevic, trans. by Monique Chefdor & Stella Harvey
Sunshine Wound by L. S. Klatt
System and Population by Christopher Sindt
There Are as Many Songs in the World as Branches of Coral by
    Elizabeth Jacobson
These Beautiful Limits by Thomas Lisk
They Who Saw the Deep by Geraldine Monk
The Thinking Eye by Jennifer Atkinson
This History That Just Happened by Hannah Craig
An Unchanging Blue: Selected Poems 1962–1975 by
    Rolf Dieter Brinkmann, trans. by Mark Terrill
Under the Quick by Molly Bendall
Verge by Morgan Lucas Schuldt
The Visible Woman by Allison Funk
The Wash by Adam Clay
Well by Sasha Steensen
We'll See by Georges Godeau, trans. by Kathleen McGookey
What Stillness Illuminated by Yermiyahu Ahron Taub
Winter Journey [Viaggio d'inverno] by Attilio Bertolucci, trans. by
    Nicholas Benson
Wonder Rooms by Allison Funk

www.ingramcontent.com/pod-product-compliance
Lightning Source LLC
LaVergne TN
LVHW091232080426
835509LV00009B/1247